Excel 365 Formatting

EASY EXCEL 365 ESSENTIALS - BOOK 1

M.L. HUMPHREY

SELECT TITLES BY M.L. HUMPHREY

EXCEL 365 ESSENTIALS
Excel 365 for Beginners
Intermediate Excel 365
102 Useful Excel 365 Functions

EASY EXCEL 365 ESSENTIALS
Formatting
Conditional Formatting
Charts
Pivot Tables
The IF Functions
XLOOKUP Functions

See mlhumphrey.com for Microsoft Word, PowerPoint and Access titles and more

CONTENTS

Introduction

This book is part of the *Easy Excel 365 Essentials* series of titles. These are targeted titles that are excerpted from the main *Excel 365 Essentials* series and are focused on one specific topic.

If you want a more general introduction to Excel, then you should check out the *Excel 365 Essentials* titles instead. In this case, *Excel 365 for Beginners* which covers formatting as well as a number of other topics, such as sorting and filtering.

But if all you want is a book that covers this specific topic, then let's continue with a discussion of your formatting options in Microsoft Excel.

Formatting

If you're going to spend any amount of time working in Excel then you need to learn how to format cells, because inevitably your column won't be as wide as you want it to be or you'll want to have a cell with red-colored text or to use bolding or italics or something that isn't Excel's default.

That's what this section is for. It's an alphabetical listing of different things you might want to do to format your data in Excel.

You can either format one cell at a time by highlighting that specific cell, or you can format multiple cells at once by highlighting all of them and then choosing your formatting option. In some cases, you can also format specific text within a cell by clicking into a cell, selecting that text, and then choosing your formatting option.

There are basically four main ways to format cells or text in current versions of Excel.

First, you can use the Home tab and click on the option you want from there.

Second, you can use the Format Cells dialogue box. Either right-click from the main workspace and select the Format Cells option from the dropdown menu or use Ctrl + 1 to open the dialogue box.

Third, you can right-click from the main workspace and use the mini formatting menu that appears above or below the dropdown menu.

Finally, some of the most popular formatting options can be applied using control shortcuts. For example, Ctrl + B to bold text, Ctrl + I to apply italics, and Ctrl + U to apply a basic underline.

Okay, let's dive right in.

Align Text

By default, text within a cell is left-aligned and bottom-aligned. This won't be noticeable at the default row height and column width, but is definitely noticeable if you change either of those enough.

The easiest way to apply alignment to a cell is to go to the Alignment section on the Home tab. There are two rows of lines there on the left-hand side that visually show your choices. The top row contains Top, Middle, and Bottom alignment choices. The second row contains Left, Center, and Right. You can choose one option from each row.

In the screenshot below I've clicked on Cell B2 where I've chosen Middle Align and Center. You can see those options selected in the Alignment section of the Home tab.

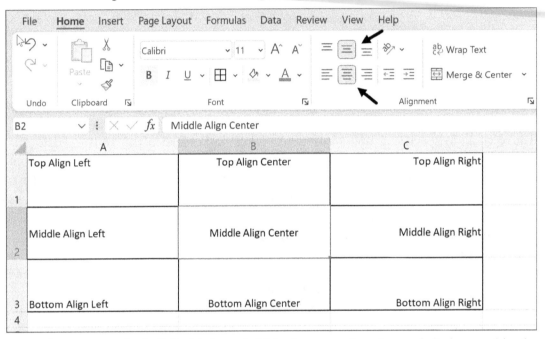

You can also see examples in Cells A1 through C3 in the screenshot above of all nine combinations.

The second-best choice for applying alignment is to use the Alignment tab of the Format Cells dialogue box. The Horizontal and Vertical alignment dropdown menus will give you the same choices as well as a few others that you're unlikely to use.

The mini formatting bar includes an option for centering your text, but that's the only alignment option it includes.

Angle Text

You can choose to angle your text in various ways using the dropdown menu under the angled "ab" with an arrow under it on the top row of the Alignment section of the Home tab.

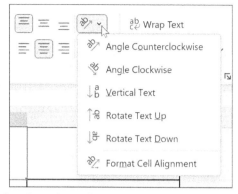

It has a handful of pre-defined options for changing the direction of text within a cell. You can choose Angle Counterclockwise, Angle Clockwise, Vertical Text, Rotate Text Up, and Rotate Text Down.

(It also offers another way to access the Alignment tab of the Format Cells dialogue box by clicking on Format Cell Alignment at the bottom of that dropdown menu.)

The Format Cells dialogue box lets you specify an exact degree for angling your text. So if you want to angle text at say a 30 degree angle, you'd need to do that in the Format Cells dialogue box. You can either enter that value in the Degrees field or click on a point in the Orientation box.

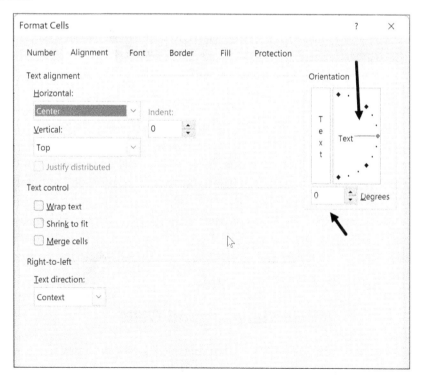

Bold Text

You can bold text in a number of ways. For each option below, select the text within a cell that you want to bold or the entire cell or cells first.

My default is to use Ctrl + B.

Another quick option is to click on the large capital B in the Font section of the Home tab.

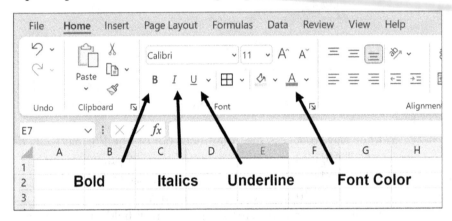

Or you can choose the capital B from the mini formatting toolbar.

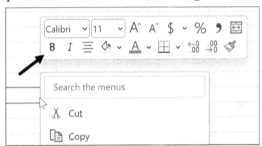

Your final option is to go to the Font tab of the Format Cells dialogue box and choose Bold from the Font Style options listing. If you want text that is both bolded and italicized, choose Bold Italic.

To remove bolding, you use the same options again (Ctrl + B or click on the capital B). If the selected text is only partially bolded when you do so, Excel will bold everything first so you'll have to do it twice. You can also go to the Format Cells dialogue box and change the Font Style to Regular.

Borders Around Cells

Placing borders around your data allows for better distinction between each cell and is something I do almost always when I create a data table. It's also very helpful when you print data from Excel, because that background grid that you see when working in Excel isn't actually present when you print.

Let me show you.

Here are those alignment choices pictured above as seen in Excel with no border around the individual cells. You can see that there is a faint line around each cell, right?

Here is the print preview of the first two columns of that image:

Note how the borders are no longer showing on the page? That's because the default cell borders that you see when working in Excel do not print. You have to add your own borders if you want your data to print with borders around it.

For the final comparison, this is that same information in print preview with a border added:

(Print preview, which we'll discuss in the chapter on how to print, is the best way to see how your data will actually appear when printed without wasting paper actually printing the document.)

There are three main ways to add borders around a cell or set of cells.

The easiest is also the newest.

If all you want is a simple basic border around a range of cells, go to the Font section on the Home tab and click on the dropdown arrow for the Borders dropdown option. It's a four-square grid with an arrow next to it that's located between the U used for underlining and the color bucket used for filling a cell with color.

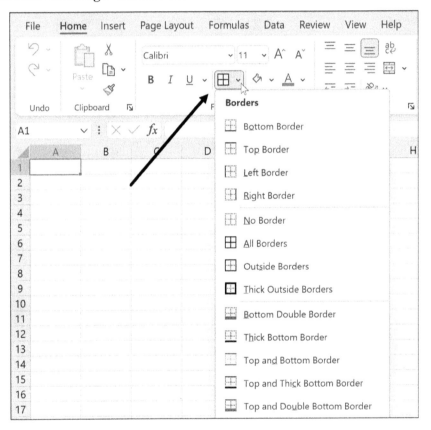

Go to the bottom of the dropdown menu and choose Draw Border Grid:

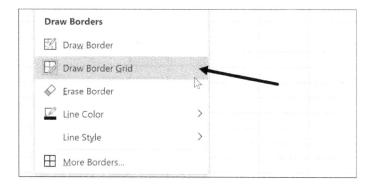

Click on it and then select the cells that you want to apply borders to.

Excel will apply the default line color and line style around all four edges of each cell you select. When you're done, use the Esc key to turn it off or click on the Border icon in the Font section of the Home tab.

For me, with the computer I'm working on and in Excel 365 as it exists in December 2022, the default line thickness isn't as dark as I would prefer it to be. I find myself wanting to change that line thickness to something I can see better on the screen.

But…

And here's where it gets weird, that line thickness is just fine in print preview. And when I choose the darker line that looks best to me on the screen, it's way too thick in print preview.

Now, I don't know if this is because of the computer I'm using which has better graphics than computers I've used in the past, or if this is part of the new streamlined appearance they rolled out with Office 2021.

But it's something to check on your own computer. Because if I were in an office environment where I was designing worksheets that others had to use and print, I'd need to be very careful that I didn't set the appearance of my worksheets to what I visually prefer since those settings will not print well.

Let me show you what I'm seeing. This is what the thick line option looks like on my worksheet:

Not bad, right? But this is what it looks like in print preview:

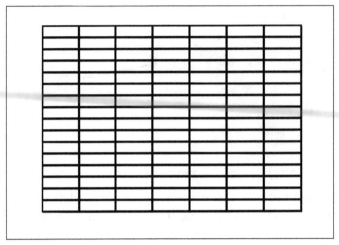

Horrible. That thick border is best for outlining a table, not for interior lines.

Which is all to say, if you're going to add borders to a document in Excel using Excel 2021 or Excel 365 and that document will be printed, be sure to look at that document in print preview before you print or provide it to others and adjust your borders accordingly.

Okay. Now, how do you adjust those lines from the default?

Go to the bottom of the Borders dropdown menu and choose one of the options from the Line Style secondary dropdown menu:

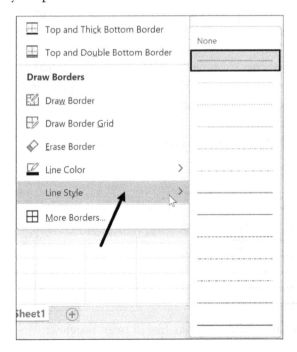

To change the line color, use the Line Color secondary dropdown menu.

The key, though, is that you need to change your line style or line color *before* you apply any borders to your cells.

That means since I don't like the default line style anymore that step one for me is to choose my line style from the dropdown. Step two is to then choose Draw Border Grid from the dropdown. Step three is to select the cells I want to add a border to. Step four is to hit Esc when I'm done.

Excel will keep that changed line style as the current default as long as that file is open.

If you have specific edges of cells where you want a border, you can use the Draw Border instead of the Draw Border Grid option. Simply select it and then click on the edge of a cell where you want to place a border line.

Draw Border when used on a range of cells at one time will apply a border around the perimeter of those selected cells but leave the inner cell borders alone.

So here, for example, I used Draw Border Grid with the default line style, highlighted my cells, and then changed the line style to the thickest option, chose Draw Border, and highlighted those exact same cells again.

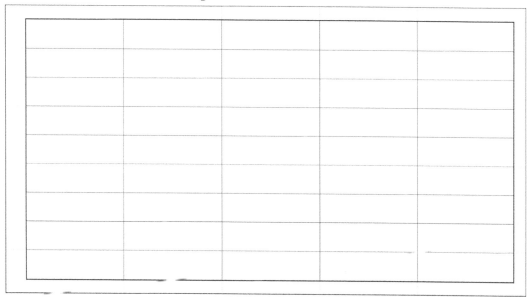

That combination gave me a table with interior lines that were thin and a dark exterior border.

Be sure each time that you choose Draw Border Grid or Draw Border that you see a pencil shape before you start highlighting your cells. There were a few times I clicked on that option and it didn't turn into the pencil for me so didn't work.

Also, hit Esc when you're done to turn off that pencil.

That is the easiest way I think to draw a table in current versions of Excel. But there are a couple other ways to do it.

That same Border dropdown menu has a number of choices at the top that you can use. With those options, though, you first need to select the cells you want to format and then choose the option you want from the dropdown.

All Borders is one I've used often as well as Thick Outside Borders. But if you use both together like I could have to create the table in the screenshot above, be sure to apply them in the right order. All Borders first, Thick Outside Borders second.

The other option for applying borders is to select your cells and then go to the Border tab of the Format Cells dialogue box either by clicking on More Borders at the bottom of the borders dropdown menu or by right-clicking on the selected cells and choosing Format Cells from that dropdown. Here is that Border tab:

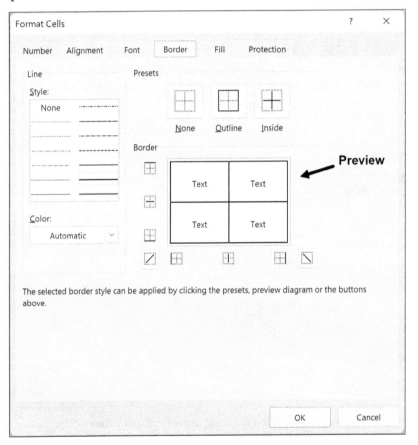

The image in the Border section of the dialogue box that shows four cells with Text in them, will show the current formatting for the selected cells.

To change that formatting, choose your line style and color on the left-hand side and then either click on the presets (none, outline, inside) above the preview or on the individual border thumbnails around the perimeter. You'll see the preview update as you click on each option.

The Format Cells dialogue box is the only way I know of to place a slanted line in a cell.

As I've done a few times in the examples above, you can combine different line styles and line colors in the same table. You just need to think through the order of applying them and make any color or line style choice first before trying to apply it to your entries.

Here is an example where I'm using three different line styles (thick, medium, and dotted line) as well as two line colors. Each of those had to be applied separately with changes to the style and/or color made before I chose the line position.

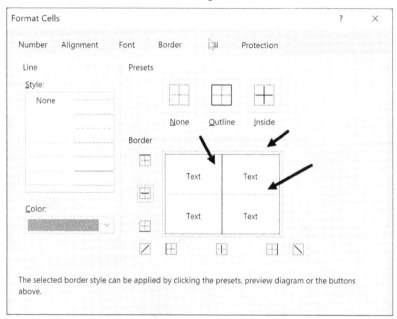

If you're in the Format Cells dialogue box and want to clear what you've done and start over, you can select None from the Presets section. The corresponding option in the dropdown menu is No Border. This does not, however, reset your line style and color choices, so if you changed those you'll need to manually change them back before you draw new borders in that worksheet. (Or close the worksheet and reopen it to reset to the default choices if you're not sure what they are.)

Color a Cell (Fill Color)

You can color (or fill) an entire cell with any color you want. I do this often when building tables. I will add fill color to the header rows of my tables and also to any columns that are either labels or non-input columns.

Like here with this example of the MAXIFS function where the header rows in each table have a green fill color, the cells with calculated results have a gray fill color, and the cells with the text of the formulas used have a blue fill color.

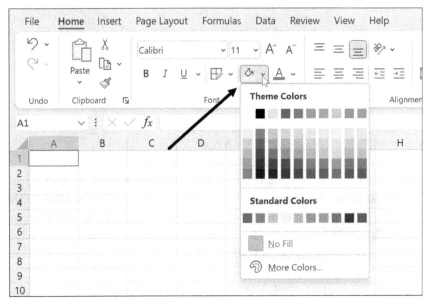

	A	B	C	D	E	F	G	H
1	Score	Teacher	Gender					
2	50	Smith	F					
3	49	Barker	M			F		M
4	68	Vasquez	F			98.00	Smith	94.00
5	75	Smith	M			90.00	Barker	93.00
6	90	Barker	F			68.00	Vasquez	76.00
7	94	Smith	M					
8	93	Barker	M			Cell F4:	=MAXIFS($A$2:$A$13,$B$2:$B$13,$G4,$C$2:$C$13,$F$3)	
9	91	Smith	F			Cell H4:	=MAXIFS($A$2:$A$13,$B$2:$B$13,$G4,$C$2:$C$13,$H$3)	
10	76	Vasquez	M					
11	82	Smith	F					
12	64	Barker	M					
13	98	Smith	F					
14								

To add fill color to a cell(s), highlight the cell(s) you want to color, go to the Font section of the Home tab, and click on the arrow to the right of the paint bucket that by default has a yellow line under it.

This should bring up a colors menu with 70 different colors to choose from, including many that are arranged as complementary themes. If you want one of those colors, just click on it.

(If you just wanted the default yellow color you could click on the paint bucket image without needing to bring up the dropdown menu. After you choose a color that option will change to show the last color used, so you can always click on the image to apply whatever color is shown without needing to use the dropdown menu.)

For more color options or to specify a specific color, click on More Colors at the bottom of the dropdown menu to bring up the Colors dialogue box.

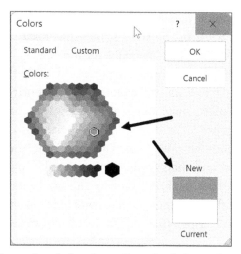 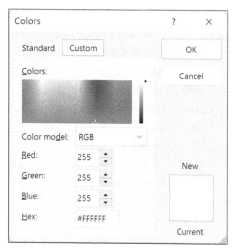

The first tab of that box, Standard, has a honeycomb-like image in the center that includes a number of colors you can choose from by clicking into the honeycomb. Shades of black, white, or gray can be selected just below that.

When you select a color it will show in the bottom right corner in the top half of the rectangle there under the heading New.

The second tab is the Custom tab. Click on it and you'll see a rectangle with a rainbow of colors that you can click on to select a color.

It also allows you to enter specific RGB, HSL, or Hex code values to get the exact color you need. (If you have a corporate color palette, for example, they should give you the values for each of the corporate colors. At least my employers always have.)

RGB is the default option, but you can change that in the dropdown menu.

Or you can enter a specific Hex code at the bottom if you have that.

On the Custom tab, you can also use the arrow on the right-hand side to darken or lighten your color.

If you like your choice, click on OK. If you don't want to add color to a cell after all, choose Cancel.

If you add Fill Color to a cell and later want to remove it, select the cell, go back to the dropdown menu, and choose the No Fill option.

Column Width

If your columns aren't the width you want, you have three options for adjusting them.

First, you can right-click on the column and choose Column Width from the dropdown menu. When the box showing you the current column width appears, enter a new column width. (I don't use this one often because I'm not a good judge of how wide I need to make a column in terms of a specific numeric value.)

Second, you can place your cursor to the right side of the column name—it should look like a line with arrows on either side when you have it in the right spot—and then left-click and drag either to the right or left until the column is as wide as you want it to be.

Or, third, you can place your cursor on the right side of the column name and double left-click. This will make the column as wide or as narrow as the widest text currently in that column. (Usually. Sometimes this one has a mind of its own. But it almost always works with shorter text entries.)

To adjust all column widths in your document at once, you can highlight the entire worksheet (Ctrl + A or click in the top left corner) and then apply one of the above options. A double-left click on any column border will adjust each column to the contents in that column. (Usually. See comment above.) Manually adjusting the width of one column or setting a Column Width using the dropdown menu, will apply that width to all columns in the worksheet.

Currency Formatting

Currency has two main formatting options, Currency and Accounting, but there are a number of other choices available as well.

To format cells using one of the currency options, highlight the cell(s) you want formatted, and then go to the Number section of the Home tab, and either click on the $ sign (which will use the Accounting format) or click on the dropdown arrow for General and choose Currency or Accounting.

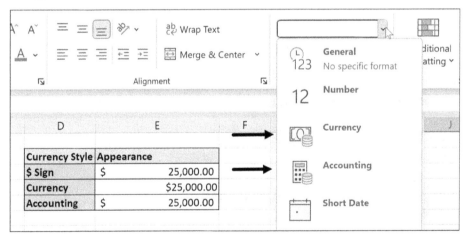

As you can see in the image above, the main difference between the two options is where they place the $ sign relative to the numbers. The Currency option places the $ sign right next to the number, the Accounting option left-aligns the $ sign and right-aligns the numbers.

The $ sign option in the Number section of the Home tab has a dropdown menu where you can choose other common currencies. Also, if you just want your currency to display as whole numbers you can click on the Decrease Decimal option twice, which is located in that same row.

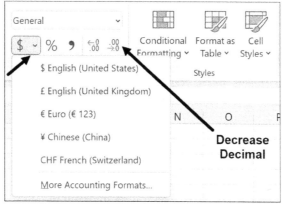

If those options aren't enough for you, you can go to the Number tab of the Format Cells dialogue box and then either use the Currency or Accounting category:

That gives a much larger range of currencies to choose from. The Currency category also includes multiple choices for how to distinguish negative values.

You can also use Ctrl + Shift + $ to apply the Currency format to a selected cell or range of cells.

Date Formatting

Not only does Excel sometimes like to format things as a date that aren't but it also sometimes has a mind of its own about how to format dates. Here are a few examples:

Input Value	Excel Default Displayed Result	Excel Short Date
3/6	6-Mar	3/6/2022
January	January	January
January 2020	Jan-20	1/1/2020
3/6/20	3/6/2020	3/6/2020

In the first column you can see the text I entered. In the second column you can see what Excel did with that text. The third column is the date, when applicable, that Excel assigned to what I'd entered.

So that first entry 3/6, Excel automatically interpreted as the date March 6th (for me, here in the United States with U.S. settings) but rewrote it as 6-Mar and added the current year to the date, which was 2022 when I was writing this so stored that date as March 6, 2022.

The second one, January, it left alone and did not turn into a date.

The third, January 2020, it converted into a date, rewrote as Jan-20, and stored as January 1, 2020.

The fourth, 3/6/20, it reformatted slightly, and treated as March 6, 2020. (Again, for me, here in the United States where month is written first.)

This demonstrates a key thing you need to remember about Excel and dates. It will always insist on having a month, day of the month, and year for every date. If you don't provide that, Excel will do it for you. And it is over-eager to turn anything that may possibly be a date into a date.

The other thing to know is that once Excel decides something is a date, you can't really change that with formatting. So with that first entry there I tried to change that to a Text format and it showed it as the number 44626 which is how Excel really stores dates behind the scenes. (As the 44,626th day since Excel's start date.)

Which means that if Excel ever turns an entry of yours into a date and you didn't want it to, the best thing is to Undo and then retype the entry using that single apostrophe at the start of the cell to keep Excel from converting the entry on you.

But let's say you did want that to be a date. How can you control the date format that Excel applies to your date?

Click on the cell with your date in it, go to the Number section of the Home tab, click on the dropdown menu which should show General by default, and then choose either Short Date or Long Date from there. You will be able to see examples of what that date will look like when chosen:

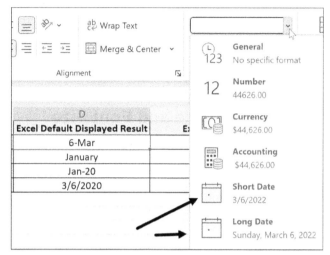

Usually, Short Date will be the one you want.

But if neither of those work for you, go to the Number tab of the Format Cells dialogue box, and click on the Date category. There will be about a dozen options to choose from there.

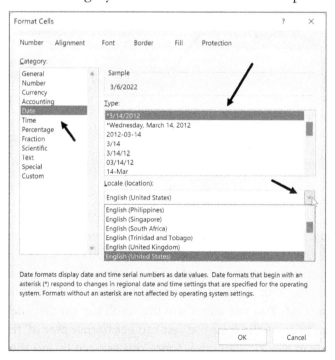

Note that there is also a Locale dropdown menu that lets you choose formats used in other countries. For example, here in the United States 3/6 is March 6th, but in many other parts of the world 3/6 is June 3rd, so if you're going to use that Short Date format understand that it is a regional format that may be misinterpreted by others on a printed document. (I believe Excel adjusts the display for the local country settings, so it won't be an issue when looking at the Excel file, but be careful there just in case.)

You can also use Ctrl + Shift + # to apply a date format that uses day, month, and year. For me the format was 2-Jan-20 for January 2, 2020.

Font Choice and Font Size

The current default font choice in Excel is Calibri and the default font size is 11 point.

You may have strong preferences about what font you use or work for a company that uses specific fonts for its brand or just want some variety in terms of font size or type within a specific document. In that case, you will need to change those settings.

There are a few ways to do this. Each requires selecting your text or cells first.

Once you've done that, option one is to go to the Font section on the Home tab and select a different font or font size from the dropdown menus there by clicking on the one you want.

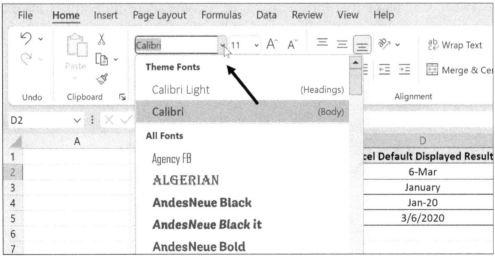

Which fonts are available in the font dropdown will depend on which fonts you have on your computer. Most people have a number of fonts already available. I have a large number of additional fonts so you may see different fonts listed there than I do.

Excel shows your theme font at the top and then the rest of your fonts are shown in alphabetical order below that. You can either use the scroll bar on the side to scroll down or you can start typing the name of the font you want to get to that part of the list.

Each font will display in the list using that font. You can see this in the screenshot above where Agency is a very different font from Andes Neue and Algerian.

The font size dropdown only has the most common sizes listed. It lists 8, 9, 10, 11, and 12 pt but then starts jumping up in numbers. If you have a specific font size you want that isn't listed, you can just type it in.

You also have the option to increase or decrease the font one listed size at a time by clicking on the A's with little arrows that are shown next to the font dropdown box. The bigger of the two, on the left, increases the font size. The smaller one decreases the font size.

All of these options are also available in the mini formatting menu if you right-click in the main workspace after selecting your cells.

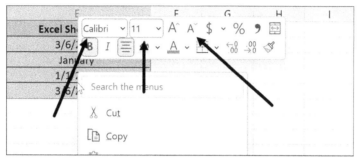

Your other option, which really doesn't give you any additional functionality, is to use the Font tab of the Format Cells dialogue box.

Font Color

The default color for all text in Excel is black, but you can change that if you want or need to. (For example, if you've filled a cell with a darker color you may want to change the font color to white to make the text in that cell more visible.)

You have three options. All require selecting the text or cells first.

After that, the first option is to go to the Font section on the Home tab and click on the arrow next to the A that by default will have a red line under it. (Or click on the A if you want the color shown.)

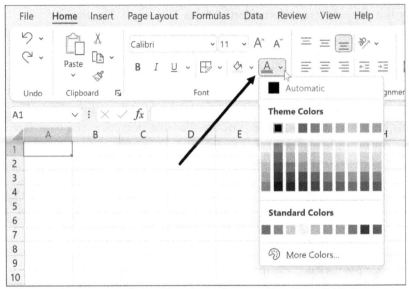

You can then choose from one of the 70 colors that are listed, and if those aren't enough of a choice you can click on More Colors and select your color from the Colors dialogue box. (See Coloring a Cell for more detail about that option.)

Second, you can use the mini formatting menu.

Third, you can use the Color dropdown in the Font tab of the Format Cells dialogue box.

Indent Text

If you want your text within your cell to be indented from the edge of the cell, you can increase the indent to make that happen by selecting the cell, going to the Alignment section of the Home tab, and clicking on the Increase Indent option that's located to the left of the Merge & Center option.

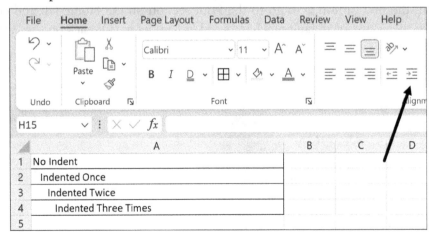

You can see how that would impact text placement in the screenshot above.

To decrease the indent, use the Decrease Indent option located to the left of the Increase Indent option.

You can also use the Indent field in the Alignment section of the Format Cells dialogue box. It will accept a whole number for the number of times to indent the text.

Italicize Text

To italicize text, highlight the text selection or cells containing text you want to italicize, and then use Ctrl + I or click on the slanted I in the Font section on the Home tab or in the mini formatting menu.

You can also change the Font Style option in the Font tab of the Format Cells dialogue box to Italic or Bold Italic.

To remove italics from text or cells that already have it, select that text and then use Ctrl + I or click on the slanted I in the Font section of the Home tab or the mini formatting menu. You may have to do this twice if you select text that is only partially italicized since Excel will apply italics to the entire selection first.

You can also remove italics by changing the Font Style back to Regular in the Format Cells dialogue box.

Merge & Center

Merge and Center is a specialized command that can come in handy when you're working with a table where you want a header that spans multiple columns of data. (Don't use it if you plan to do a lot of data analysis with what you've input into the worksheet because it will mess with your ability to filter, sort, or use pivot tables. It's really for creating a finalized, pretty-looking report.)

What it does is merges the cells you select and then centers your text across those merged cells.

You can merge cells across columns and down rows. So you could, for example, merge four cells that span two columns and two rows into one big cell while keeping all of the other cells in those columns and rows separate. But what I usually am doing is just merging X number of cells in a single row.

If you're going to merge and center cells that contain text, make sure that the text you want to keep is in the top-most and left-most of the cells you plan to merge and center. Data in the other cells that are being merged will be deleted. (You'll get a warning message to this effect if you have values in any of the other cells.)

To use this option, first select all of the cells you want to merge.

Next, go to the Alignment section of the Home tab and choose Merge & Center. This will combine your selected cells into one cell and center the contents from that left-uppermost cell across the selection.

Like so:

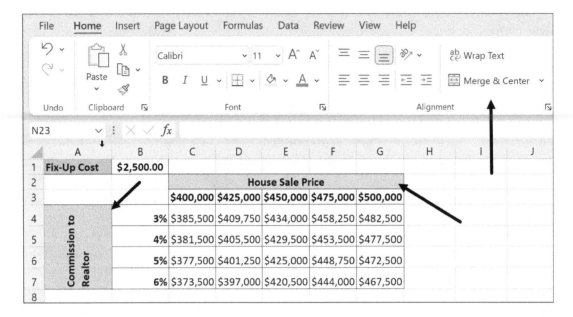

In the screenshot above I've merged and centered the text "House Sale Price" across Columns C through G in Row 2. I've also merged and centered the text "Commission to Realtor" across Rows 4 through 7 in Column A. (You'll note that I also changed the alignment of the commission text.)

That is the option I use most often, but there are additional choices available if you click on the dropdown arrow for Merge & Center. You can also choose to Merge Across (which will merge the cells in each row of the selected range separately and will not center the text) or to Merge Cells (which will merge all of the selected cells but won't center the text).

If you ever need to unmerge merged cells you can do so by selecting those cells and then clicking on the Unmerge Cells option from that dropdown.

You can also merge or unmerge cells by using the Merge Cells checkbox in the Alignment tab of the Format Cells dialogue box.

Merge & Center is also an option in the mini formatting menu. It's located in the top right corner of the menu. Clicking on it for previously merged cells will unmerge those cells.

Number Formatting

In addition to date and currency formatting, which we already discussed, you can apply other basic number formatting to your cells.

The first option is to use the Number section of the Home tab. The second option is to use the mini formatting menu. And the final option is to use the Format Cells dialogue box.

There are three default number styles in the dropdown menu on the Home tab that you may want to consider. If you already have values entered, the dropdown menu will show you a sample of how each one will look.

Here, for example, I used 10000 as my entry and you can see how General, Number, and Scientific would display that number:

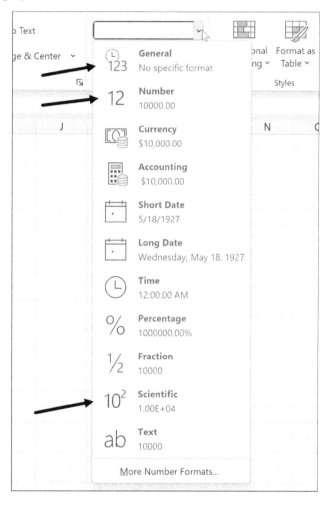

I often prefer to use the Comma Style option that's available below the dropdown and is just shown as a big comma because that one includes a comma for thousands where Number does not:

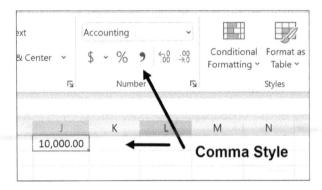

It is also available in the mini formatting menu.

Ctrl + Shift + exclamation mark (!) will give a similar but not identical result to the Comma Style option. (The spacing within the cell is different.)

And, as with all other number formatting options, there is a more detailed option in the Number section of the Format Cells dialogue box, in this case using the Number category.

You can also use the Increase and Decrease Decimal options in the Number section of the Home tab or in the mini formatting menu to change the number of decimal places for your values, just be sure to do that after you've applied your number format, not before.

Percent Formatting

To format numbers as a percentage, your first option is to highlight the cell(s), and click on the percent sign in the Number section of the Home tab or the mini formatting menu. This will convert the value to a percent with no decimal places.

Your second option is to use the dropdown menu in the Number section of the Home tab and choose Percentage from there. This will format the value as a percentage, but also include two decimal places.

Your final option is to use the Percentage category in the Number tab of the Format Cells dialogue box which will let you specify the number of decimal places to use.

With any of the above options, be sure that your numbers are formatted correctly or it won't work properly. In other words, 0.5 will translate to 50% but 50 will translate to 5000% so you want your entries pre-formatting to be .5 not 50 if you're looking for 50%.

(You can fix this by dividing those entries by 100, copying that result, and then pasting special values over the original values.)

Row Height

If your rows aren't the correct height, you have three options for adjusting them.

First, you can right-click on the row you want to adjust, choose Row Height from the dropdown menu, and when the box showing you the current row height appears, enter a new row height.

Second, you can place your cursor along the lower border of the row number for the row you want to adjust until it looks like a line with arrows above and below. Left-click and hold while you move the cursor up or down until the row is as tall as you want it to be.

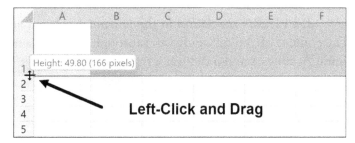

Third, you can place your cursor along the lower border of the row, and double left-click. This will fit the row height to the text in the cell. (Usually. Sometimes in the past it would not work with really large amounts of text and the only option was to manually resize the row height.)

To adjust all row heights in your document at once, highlight the entire worksheet (Ctrl + A or click in the top left corner) first and then use one of the options above. Entering a specific row height or clicking and dragging will keep all rows the same height. Double-left-clicking will resize each row to its contents. (Theoretically.)

Underline Text

Underlining text works much the same way that bolding and italics work.

For a basic single-line underline select the text or cells with text that you want to underline and then use Ctrl + U or click on the underlined U in the Font section of the Home tab.

You can also use the Underline dropdown in the Font section of the Format Cells dialogue box.

There are other underline types such as a double underline. For that, use the dropdown arrow next to the underlined U in the Font section of the Home tab or choose one of the options in the Format Cells dialogue box which includes single accounting and double accounting options as well.

To remove underlining from text or cells that already have it, highlight the text and then use one of the above options again. If you applied a special underline type, then using Ctrl + U or clicking on the underlined U in the Font section will first change the underline to a single underline, so you have to do it twice to completely remove the underline.

Wrap Text

Wrap text is an essential one to learn if you want to use text in your worksheet and be able to see all of the text in that worksheet without expanding the width of your columns to make that happen.

To Wrap Text in a cell, select the cell(s), go to the Alignment section of the Home Tab, and click on the Wrap Text option in the top row.

Or you can go to the Alignment tab in the Format Cells dialogue box and check the box for Wrap Text in the Text Control section.

Here is an example of a FINRA regulation in the left-most column and then an analysis column next to it. The content of the cells in Rows 1 through 3 are the same as those in Rows 6 through 8. In Column A, Rows 2 and 3 did not wrap the text but Rows 7 and 8 did.

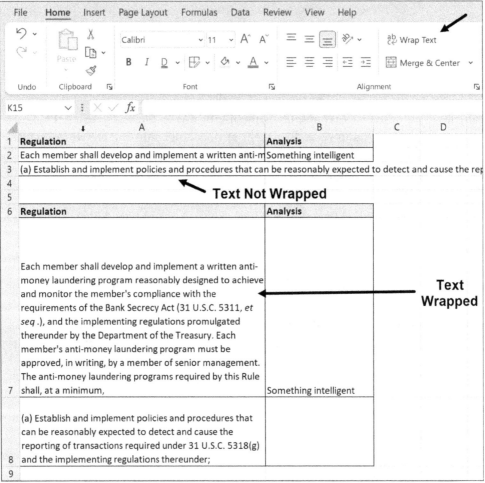

Note a few things. In the example at the top where the text is not wrapped, the text stops at the next column when there is content in that next column. You can see that in Cell A2. But when there isn't text in that next column, the text is visible on the screen. You can see that in Cell A3.

But when text is wrapped, like in Cells A7 and A8, the text moves to a new line when it reaches the border with the next column and as long as the row height is high enough, you can see the full text in that cell, regardless of what text may or may not be in any other column.

It also just looks much better when it's contained to the cell it belongs to.

(Excel does seem to have a maximum row height which will limit the amount of text you can display in one cell, so if you have any cells with lots of text in them, check to make sure that the full contents of the cell are actually visible. You may have to manually adjust the row height or it just may not be possible to see all of the text.)

$$* * *$$

Okay. That was our alphabetical discussion of the various formatting options, but before we move on to sorting and filtering, I wanted to cover a couple more formatting tricks.

Copy Formatting From One Cell To Another

I find this one incredibly useful, although I use it more in Word than in Excel.

If you already have a cell formatted the way you want it, you can use the Format Painter located in the Clipboard section of the Home tab to sweep the formatting from that cell to other cells you want formatted the same way.

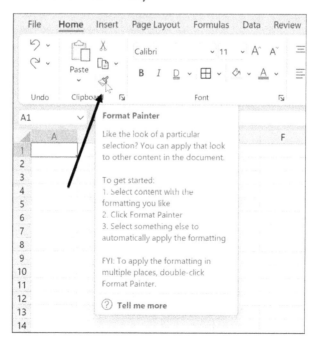

The help text sort of says it all.

First, select the cell(s) that have the formatting you want to copy (if the formatting is identical, just highlight one cell).

Next, click on the Format Painter. Double-click if you have more than one place you want to apply that formatting.

Finally, click into the cell(s) you want to copy the formatting to.

The contents in the destination cell will remain the same, but the font, font color, font size, cell borders, italics/bolding/underlining, and text alignment and orientation will all change to match that of the cell that you swept the formatting from.

If you double-clicked, use Esc or click on the Format Painter again to turn it off when you're done.

You can also find the Format Painter tool in the mini formatting menu.

You need to be careful using the Format Painter because it will change all formatting in your destination cells. So, if the cell you're copying the formatting from is bolded and has red text, both of those attributes will copy over even if all you were trying to do was copy the bold formatting. (This is more of a problem when using the tool in Word than in Excel, but it's still something to watch out for especially if you have borders around cells.)

Also, the tool copies formatting to whatever cell you select next, which can be a problem if the cell you're copying from isn't next to the one you're copying to. DO NOT use arrow keys to navigate between the cells. You need to click directly on the cell you're transferring the formatting to.

Remember, Ctrl + Z is your friend if you make a mistake. But if you format sweep and then undo, you'll see that the cell(s) you were trying to format from are surrounded by a dotted border as if you had copied the cells. Be sure to hit the Esc key before you continue to turn that off.

Clear Formatting

I don't use this often, but it can be handy if I had a lot of formatting in a worksheet and deleted the contents but the formatting is still there and I don't want it anymore.

To clear formatting, select the cells where you want to do this (or the entire worksheet with Ctrl + A), and then go to the Editing section of the Home tab and click on the dropdown arrow under Clear.

The Clear Formats option will remove all formatting from the selected cells. Clear All will remove contents and formatting at the same time.

Appendix A: Basic Terminology

These terms are defined in detail in *Excel 365 for Beginners*. This is just a quick overview in case it's needed.

Workbook

A workbook is what Excel likes to call an Excel file.

Worksheet

Excel defines a worksheet as the primary document you use in Excel to store and work with your data. A worksheet is organized into Columns and Rows that form Cells. A workbook can contain multiple worksheets.

Columns

Excel uses columns and rows to display information. Columns run across the top of the worksheet and, unless you've done something funky with your settings, are identified using letters of the alphabet.

The first column in a worksheet will always be Column A. And the number of columns in your worksheet will remain the same, regardless of how many columns you delete, add, or move around. Think of columns as location information that is actually separate from the data in the worksheet.

Rows

Rows run down the side of each worksheet and are numbered starting at 1 and up to a very high number. Row numbers are also locational information. The first row will always be numbered 1, the second row will always be numbered 2, and so on and so forth. There will also always be a fixed number of rows in each worksheet regardless of how many rows of data you delete, add, or move around.

Cells

Cells are where the row and column data comes together. Cells are identified using the letter for the column and the number for the row that intersect to form that cell. For example, Cell A1 is the cell that is in the first column and first row of the worksheet.

Click

If I tell you to click on something, that means to use your mouse (or trackpad) to move the cursor on the screen over to a specific location and left-click or right-click on the option. If you left-click, this selects the item. If you right-click, this generally displays a dropdown list of options to choose from. If I don't tell you which to do, left- or right-click, then left-click.

Left-click/Right-click

If you look at your mouse you generally have two flat buttons to press. One is on the left side, one is on the right. If I say left-click that means to press down on the button on the left. If I say right-click that means press down on the button on the right.

Select

If I tell you to "select" cells, that means to highlight them. You can either left-click and drag to select a range of cells or hold down the Ctrl key as you click on individual cells. To select an entire column, click on the letter for the column. To select an entire row, click on the number for the row.

Data

Data is the information you enter into your worksheet.

Data Table

I may also sometimes refer to a data table or table of data. This is just a combination of cells that contain data in them.

Arrow

If I tell you to arrow to somewhere or to arrow right, left, up, or down, this just means use the arrow keys to navigate to a new cell.

Cursor Functions

The cursor is what moves around when you move your mouse or use the trackpad. In Excel the cursor changes its appearance depending on what functions you can perform.

Tab

I am going to talk a lot about Tabs, which are the options you have to choose from at the top of the workspace. The default tab names are File, Home, Insert, Page Layout, Formulas, Data, Review, View, and Help. But there are certain times when additional tabs will appear, for example, when you create a pivot table or a chart.

(This should not be confused with the Tab key which can be used to move across cells.)

Dropdown Menus

A dropdown menu is a listing of available choices that you can see when you right-click in certain places such as the main workspace or on a worksheet name. You will also see them when you click on an arrow next to or below an option in the top menu.

Dialogue Boxes

Dialogue boxes are pop-up boxes that contain additional choices.

Scroll Bars

When you have more information than will show in a screen, dialogue box, or dropdown menu, you will see scroll bars on the right side or bottom that allow you to navigate to see the rest of the information.

Formula Bar

The formula bar is the long white bar at the top of the main workspace directly below the top menu options that lets you see the actual contents of a cell, not just the displayed value.

Cell Notation

Cells are referred to by their column and row position. So Cell A1 is the cell that's the intersection of the first column and first row in the worksheet.

When written in Excel you just use A1, you do not need to include the word cell. A colon (:) can be used to reference a range of cells. A comma (,) can be used to separate cell references.

When in doubt about how to define a cell range, click into a cell, type =, and then go and select the cells you want to reference. Excel will describe your selection in the formula bar using cell notation.

Paste Special Values

Paste Special Values is a way of pasting copied values that keeps the calculation results or the cell values but removes any formulas or formatting.

Task Pane

On occasion Excel will open a task pane, which is different from a dialogue box because it is part of the workspace. These will normally appear on the right-hand side in Excel for tasks such as working with pivot tables or charts or using the built-in Help function. (They often appear on the left-hand side in Word.)

They can be closed by clicking on the X in the top right corner.

About the Author

M.L. Humphrey is a former stockbroker with a degree in Economics from Stanford and an MBA from Wharton who has spent close to twenty years as a regulator and consultant in the financial services industry.

You can reach M.L. at mlhumphreywriter@gmail.com or at mlhumphrey.com.

* * *

If you want to learn more about Microsoft Excel, check out *Excel Tips and Tricks* or one of the main Excel 365 Essentials titles, *Excel 365 for Beginners*, *Intermediate Excel 365*, or *102 Useful Excel 365 Functions*.